AYURVEDA WINTER WELLNESS 101

SEASONAL NUTRITION & SELF HEALING
PRACTICES FOR EACH DOSHA.

Written By

PURETURE, HHP

PURETURE
HEALING THE FUTURE WITH PURE NATURE

CONTENTS

INTRODUCTION

You might not know this, but energetic disruptions in your life forces can lead to illness. That's why it's imperative to understand how to maintain harmony in your system through every season of the year. You can do that using Ayurveda practices that not only help you maintain energetic balance but also pave the way to heal yourself from disruptions. What is Ayurveda?

Ayurvedic medicine is an ancient healing system that has been practiced for more than 3,000 years. Ayurvedic practitioners understand that there is a delicate balance between your mind, body, and spirit, and the key to your health is maintaining that balance. The focus of Ayurveda is to promote good health through preventative medical practices, but the techniques can also be used to fight disease. The philosophical foundation of this kind of medicine is the fact that everything is connected. If your mind, body, and spirit are all in harmony, you will experience good health. However, when something happens that disrupts that delicate balance, illness can result.

Another fundamental principle of Ayurveda is that every living person is made up of combinations of elements. These elements include space, air, fire, water, and earth, and they combine to form the three life forces, which are also known as doshas. The three doshas are Vata (space and air), Pitta (fire and water), and Kapha (water and earth). Every individual comprises a unique mix of the three doshas, and each dosha controls different body functions. Of the three doshas, Vata is the most powerful, and as such, it is in control of your mind, breathing, blood flow, heart function, and the ability of your body to eliminate waste. Fear or grief can disrupt this powerful dosha, but so can more minor things like staying up too late or eating too soon after a meal. A disruption in this dosha can result in anxiety, heart disease, asthma, skin problems, and rheumatoid arthritis.

The Pitta dosha has control over your metabolism, digestion, and the hormones that control your appetite. This life force can be disrupted by spicy or sour foods or spending too much time in the sun. A disruption in this dosha can result in Crohn's disease, high blood pressure, heart disease, and infections. The third dosha, Kapha, controls muscle growth, body stability, and strength. It also has control over your immune system and your weight. The kinds of behaviors that can cause a disruption include sleeping during the day, eating too many sweets, or eating foods that have too much salt or water. Disruptions can result in cancer, diabetes, nausea after eating, certain breathing disorders, obesity, and asthma.

When Ayurvedic medical practitioners treat disruptions in your life forces, they take your unique physical and emotional makeup, primary life force, and the balance of the three doshas before creating an individual treatment plan for your specific needs. The goal of the treatment is to cleanse your body of undigested food. This is accomplished using a process called panchakarma and is designed to restore harmony and balance so that your symptoms will be reduced as the illness is resolved. The techniques they use include things like blood purification, massage, medical oils, herbs, enemas, and laxatives. However, you can also use a variety of techniques to heal yourself. That's the purpose of this book--to show you how to heal imbalances and maintain harmony in your doshas all in your own home's privacy.

I know the techniques presented in this book can help you because I also suffered from Western medication's health conditions. I used these techniques to cure myself, and that's why I know these holistic techniques can work for you too. My own health experiences led me to become a holistic health practitioner, a yoga practitioner, a personal fitness trainer, and a mindfulness enthusiast. Ayurveda medicine helped me heal myself, which prompted me to do some more research to create a series of books to help people, like yourself, who are suffering too. I have been doing this for well over a decade now as of writing the series and am passionate about passing on my knowledge. To help me do that, I created Pureture Wellness with the mission of helping you reach your optimal wellness through natural, holistic, and alternative medicine techniques like Ayurveda.

This book is part of a series of four books about balancing your doshas in each season of the year. This book focuses on the Ayurveda practices you can use to heal disruptions and maintain balance in the winter. What does winter have to do with it? Quite simply, your doshas interact with each season differently, so you have to change your strategies throughout the year to stay balanced. Winter and autumn are the seasons of Vata. If this is your dominant dosha, you're likely to be adventurous, dreamy, bubbly, charismatic and creative, artistic, and inspirational. You're also more likely to be affected by the winter season than the other dosha types.

Pitta is associated with summer, and if it's your dominant dosha, you probably have a clear vision and are full of energy and passion. Kapha is the dosha associated with spring, and those whose primary dosha is Kapha are patient, understanding, calm, and easily able to remember even minor details. If you want to know your dominant dosha, there are several websites with tests that can help you determine that. It's a good idea to find that out since you'll know the specific strategies to use for each season of the year. This book will discuss the effects of the winter season on the three doshas, provide self-healing techniques and methods to maintain balance all year long.

Recommendation from the Pureture Wellness team:

We would like to make this journey you are about to embark on as smooth as possible with some extra tips and resources that you could find very useful when it comes to creating more balance. As with any journey, preparations need to be made, and there are tools fit for each pilgrimage. In our case we recommend the Detox Goodies Toolkit, which is completely free. In this toolkit you will find 20 amazing detox tips that you can implement daily. Many of the tips in this toolkit are based from Ayurvedic practices, easy to implement and overall feel really good. There are additional pieces of information, however it is worth mentioning that they are not geared for specific doshas.

Please access the following link: https://www.pureture.com/detox-goodies/

In this link you will find the following components:

- 20 Daily Detox Tips
- 15 Detox Tea Formulas

- 10 Detox Juices
- Master Shopping List: Healing & Detox Food

So, if you're ready to embark on a holistic self-healing, energy-balancing journey, let's get started with nutrition for each of the doshas in the winter season!

1

PITTA NUTRITION FOR STAYING BALANCED IN WINTER

T he Pitta dosha is fiery, and if it's your primary dosha, you run hotter than other people, literally. Your body temperature will run hotter (not feverish, but warmer). That means you'll be better able to withstand cold temperatures, and you'll have better digestive capability and a hardier appetite. On the other hand, you can also be a little hot-headed at times since you're more aggressive and impatient than any of the other types. You're also brilliant and quick-witted. Your diet can include almost anything, but you are prone to use too much salt, sour, and spicy foods, and you can sometimes overeat. Let's look at some specific Pitta qualities.

Pitta Qualities

Pitta's primary function is transformation, just like fire, and that's why it's associated with the same kinds of fire qualities.

These include heat, light, intensity, pungent, sharp, acidic, or penetrating qualities. Because it is associated with transformation, Pitta is in control of digestion, metabolism, and energy production. That makes sense since your digestive system is transforming food into energy that your body can use as fuel. Let's look at some of the specific characteristics associated with this dosha:

- **Physical Characteristics:** Pitta's physical characteristics include a warmer than normal temperature, which goes along with having an excess of energy. All that energy enables you to sleep soundly, but only for short periods. You also tend to have a great appetite. When you're out of balance, you can experience various problems like rashes, burning sensations, peptic ulcers, indigestion, heartburn, and excessive body heat.

- **Emotional Characteristics:** Emotionally, Pittas are formidable intellects, and they excel at concentration. Those qualities mean they're excellent at making decisions, teaching, and speaking. Pittas are also outspoken, quick-witted, precise, and direct, which makes them very ambitious and practical. They love a challenge and are always up for a thrilling adventure. When they're unbalanced, they can be argumentative, short-tempered, and they might also experience the occasional emotional outburst.

You might be starting to see why staying balanced is so important, but how do you do that? Since Pitta is associated with fire, you want to balance that by keeping calm. Get plenty of fresh air and choose cooler times of the day to work out. You also want to stay physically and mentally relaxed and collected. That means do everything in moderation. Also, stay out of those situations where you might be exposed to excessive heat, steam, or humidity.

Moreover, be sure to drink plenty of fluids. It can also help to practice keeping your cool by participating in quiet, contemplative activities and avoiding situations where you're exposed to conflict. It's also critical to follow a specific diet plan that takes the year's season into account. Let's take a look at what that means.

Favorable Foods

Since Pitta is fiery, it's better in general to consume foods that are warm or cool rather than excessively hot or cold. You also want to choose foods with moderately heavy textures. Bitter, sweet, and astringent tastes like mint or licorice are the best for this dosha, and red meat generates a lot of heat, so it's better to stick to a vegetarian diet or consume other types of meat. Even then, you should minimize the amount of meat in general. Milk, grains, and vegetables are better than meat for a Pitta. These are general recommendations, but the cold, heavy, and slow winter qualities are an excellent balance to Pitta's internal fire and the sharp, penetrating nature of the Pitta mind. So, what are the specific dietary recommendations for winter?

Foods to Favor In Winter

In winter, Pittas should consume more warm, cooked, and well-spiced foods that feature a balance of Pitta's tastes and are only slightly oily. For vegetables, choose from asparagus, green beans, leeks, okra, and rutabaga for the best support, and among fruits, berries, soaked prunes, and soaked raisins are great for staying balanced. Amaranth, basmati rice and seitan are some of the best grains for the Pitta body, and for dairy, ghee and warm milk work best. Pittas typically want to choose soothing spices, but they can choose from more options in the winter. Cardamom, cinnamon, fresh ginger, mint, parsley, saffron, tarragon, turmeric, and vanilla are suitable for keeping Pitta balanced in the winter. Herbal tea made from cumin, coriander, and fennel is perfect for Pitta as are sunflower seeds, which can be eaten year-round.

Acceptable Winter Indulgences

Since winter is an excellent seasonal balance for Pittas, it's one time of year when they can indulge in certain foods that might otherwise be too much for their fiery nature. These include eggs, meats, caffeinated teas, coffee or espresso, and spices that add more fire to your meals. It's also okay during this time to indulge in an occasional glass of dry, red wine. Hot, spiced chai or maple tapioca makes for great sweet treats.

Foods to Minimize

There are some foods that you specifically want to minimize or even avoid in the winter if you're a Pitta type. You can eat fruits like bananas, cranberries, grapes, grapefruit, pineapple, and tamarind in moderation, but you want to keep them to a minimum. It's also a good idea to cut down on cooked spinach, hard cheeses, miso, and sour cream. You also want to minimize fermented foods, trikatu, and herbal teas that contain dried ginger, cinnamon, clove, or black pepper. This is particularly true if you tend toward excess acidity.

Lifestyle Adjustments

Because Pitta's life embodies a sharp sense of focus and purpose, it's a good idea to balance that by relaxing your expectations, slowing down, and being more receptive to the winter season's gentleness. This will help to ease you into the softness of the season. You'll also benefit from a routine and spending time cultivating stillness and solitude. A morning oil massage is a valuable part of your routine, and you might also consider the following pranayama practices:

- Nadi Shodhana--alternate nostril breathing;
- Kapalabhati--skull shining breath;
- Bhastrika--bellows breath.

In your yoga practice, you'll want to incorporate standing poses and twists, and forward bends will help you nurture a sense of surrender--see Chapter Four for some specific poses and instructions on how to achieve them. The cold weather of winter will allow you to push yourself a bit harder, but you should still practice releasing any attachment you have to a certain performance level. Try to maintain a relaxed effort attitude instead. Try to end your days by retiring close to 10 PM, and it's helpful to rise with the sun.

Winter Eating Guideline for Pitta

The following presents some specific food guidelines for Pitta in the wintertime. We'll look at the best foods to eat for each category.

Fruits

Sweet, somewhat astringent fruits are best for Pitta types. Dried fruits are also okay, but you should consume those in moderation to accelerate your already natural tendency toward rapid digestion. Pittas should avoid fruits that heat the body or that are sour, such as bananas, cranberries, and green grapes. It's also a smart idea to enjoy fruits and fruit juices alone, meaning without any other food. You should wait at least thirty minutes, ideally for one hour, before eating different food types. That will help ensure you don't encounter any digestion problems. You should note that the "30-minute rule" doesn't apply to those kinds of fruits that we typically consider vegetables, like avocados, cucumbers, and tomatoes. The following is a list of fruits to favor and avoid for Pittas:

Favor	Avoid
• Apples (sweet)	• Apples (sour)
• Applesauce	• Apricots (sour)
• Apricots (sweet)	• Bananas
• Berries (sweet)	• Berries (sour)
• Cherries (sweet)	• Cherries (sour)
• Coconut	• Cranberries
• Dates	• Grapefruit
• Figs	• Grapes (green)
• Grapes (red, purple, black)	• Kiwi
• Limes	• Lemons
• Mangos (ripe)	• Mangos (green)
• Melons	• Oranges (sour)
• Oranges (sweet)	• Peaches
• Papaya	• Persimmons
• Pears	• Pineapple (sour)
• Pineapple (sweet)	• Plums (sour)
• Plums (sweet)	• Tamarind
• Pomegranates	
• Prunes	
• Raisins	
• Strawberries	
• Watermelon	

Vegetables

For a Pitta, vegetables that are sweet and either bitter, astringent, or both are more pacifying. Several vegetables have a combination of these tastes, so you're free to experiment with various vegetables that will help diversify your diet. For a Pitta, it's easier to digest vegetables than it is for the other doshas, but it's better to eat them midday since that's when your digestion is at peak strength. Vegetables that Pittas should avoid include spicy, sharp, sour, or heating vegetables like garlic, green chilies, radishes, mustard greens, and onions. Below is a list of vegetables to favor and avoid for Pittas:

Favor	Avoid
• Avocado	• Beet Greens
• Artichoke	• Beets (raw)
• Asparagus	• Burdock Root
• Beets (cooked)	• Corn (fresh)
• Bell Peppers	• Daikon Radish
• Bitter Melon	• Eggplant
• Broccoli	• Garlic
• Brussels Sprouts	• Green Chilies
• Cabbage	• Horseradish
• Carrots (cooked)	• Kohlrabi
• Cauliflower	• Leeks (raw)
• Celery	• Mustard Greens
• Cilantro	• Olives (green)
• Collard Greens	• Onions (raw)
• Cucumber	• Peppers (hot)
• Dandelion Greens	• Radishes (raw)
• Green Beans	• Spinach (cooked)
• Jerusalem Artichoke	• Tomatoes
• Kale	• Turnip greens
• Leafy Greens	• Turnips
• Leeks (cooked)	
• Lettuce	
• Mushrooms	
• Okra	
• Olives (black)	
• Onions (cooked)	
• Parsley	
• Parsnips	
• Peas	
• Peppers (sweet)	
• Potatoes	
• Pumpkin	
• Radishes (cooked)	
• Rutabaga	
• Spaghetti Squash	
• Sprouts (not spicy)	
• Squash, Summer	
• Squash, Winter	
• Spinach (raw)	
• Sweet Potatoes	
• Watercress	
• Wheat Grass	
• Zucchini	

Grains

Like fruits, the best grains for a Pitta are cooling, sweet, dry, and grounding. Since grains are dietary staples, Pittas get a significant benefit from their sweet, nourishing nature. To offset Pitta's oily nature, beneficial grains are dry, and if you're a Pitta, you'll want to avoid those grains that heat you up, such as buckwheat, corn, brown rice, millet, and yeasted bread. Below is a list of grains to favor and avoid for Pitta:

Favor	Avoid
• Amaranth	• Buckwheat
• Barley	• Corn
• Cereal (dry)	• Millet
• Couscous	• Muesli
• Crackers	• Polenta
• Durham Flour	• Rice (brown)
• Granola	• Rye
• Oat Bran	• Yeasted Bread
• Oats	
• Pancakes	
• Pasta	
• Quinoa	
• Rice (basmati, white, wild)	
• Rice Cakes	
• Seitan	
• Spelt	
• Sprouted Wheat Bread	
• Tapioca	
• Wheat	
• Wheat Bran	

Legumes

Like fruits and grains, Pitta's best legumes are those that are astringent, and happily, that means most are acceptable. Beans that are not appropriate for this dosha are sour or oily; these will only heat you up, which is undesirable. Below is a list of legumes to favor and avoid:

Favor	Avoid
● Adzuki Beans	● Miso
● Black Beans	● Soy Meats
● Black-Eyed Peas	● Soy Sauce
● Garbanzo Beans (Chickpeas)	● Urad Dal
● Kidney Beans	
● Lentils	
● Lima Beans	
● Mung Beans	
● Mung Dal	
● Navy Beans	
● Pinto Beans	
● Split Peas	
● Soy Beans	
● Soy Cheese	
● Soy Flour	
● Soy Milk	
● Soy Powder	
● Tempeh	
● Tofu	
● White Beans	

Dairy

In general, dairy products are grounding, nourishing, and cooling, which makes them ideal for Pitta. The ones to avoid are sour, salty, or heating. Additionally, it is best if you generally consume dairy milk one hour before or after other food. Almond and rice milk make adequate substitutes if you're lactose intolerant or need to combine milk with other foods. Below is a list of dairy foods to favor and avoid:

Favor	Avoid
• Butter (unsalted) • Cheese (soft, unsalted, not aged) • Cottage Cheese • Cow's Milk • Ghee • Goat's Milk • Goat's Cheese (soft, unsalted) • Ice Cream • Yogurt (homemade, diluted, without fruit)	• Butter (salted) • Buttermilk • Cheese (hard) • Frozen Yogurt • Sour Cream • Yogurt (store-bought, or with fruit)

Nuts & Seeds

In general, nuts and seeds are very oily, and that heats Pittas up, but there are a few types of nuts and a variety of seeds that are acceptable in small quantities. These are the less oily varieties that are either only mildly heating or even cooling in nature. Below is a list of nuts and seeds to favor and avoid:

Favor	Avoid
• Almonds (soaked and peeled)	• Almonds (with skin)
• Charole Nuts	• Brazil Nuts
• Coconut	• Cashews
• Flax Seeds	• Chia Seeds
• Halva	• Filberts
• Popcorn (buttered, without salt)	• Macadamia Nuts
• Pumpkin Seeds	• Peanuts
• Sunflower Seeds	• Pecans
	• Pine Nuts
	• Pistachios
	• Sesame Seeds
	• Tahini
	• Walnut

Meat and Eggs

Animals that are sweet, relatively dry, and only mildly heating or even cooling in nature, such as rabbit and venison, are usually better for Pittas. Meats that are oily, salty, or heating--like dark chicken, beef, salmon, or tuna--don't work well for Pittas. Below is a list of meats to favor and avoid:

Favor	Avoid
• Buffalo	• Beef
• Chicken (white)	• Chicken (dark)
• Eggs (white only)	• Duck
• Fish (freshwater)	• Eggs (yolk)
• Rabbit	• Fish (saltwater)
• Shrimp	• Lamb
• Turkey (white)	• Pork
• Venison	• Salmon
	• Sardines
	• Seafood
	• Tuna Fish
	• Turkey (dark)

Oils

Pittas can have a moderate amount of oil as long as it is a cooling type. The very best ones that work for Pittas are sunflower oil, ghee, coconut oil, and olive oil. However, if you're going to consume the favorable oils, you want to buy organic since toxins accumulate in fats. Below is a table of oils to favor and avoid:

Favor	Avoid
● Coconut Oil	● Almond Oil
● Flaxseed Oil	● Apricot Oil
● Ghee	● Corn Oil
● Olive Oil	● Safflower Oil
● Primrose Oil	● Sesame Oil
● Sunflower Oil	
● Soy Oil	
● Walnut Oil	

Sweeteners

Pittas are soothed by sweet tastes, so most sweeteners are fine, but some just heat you too much or are over-processed. Naturally occurring sweets are better than sugary sweets, but even the appropriate sweeteners are to be used in moderation. Below is a list of sweets to favor and those to avoid:

Favor	Avoid
● Barley Malt	● Honey
● Date Sugar	● Jaggery
● Fructose	● Molasses
● Fruit Juice Concentrates	● White Sugar
● Maple Syrup	
● Rice Syrup	
● Sucanat	
● Turbinado	

Spices

Most spices add too much heat for Pittas, but some are only mildly heating and help maintain a balanced digestive fire without being too irritating. Some spices have a cooling effect, such as cardamom, cilantro, coriander, fennel, and mint. There are also some spices that, although they can cause excess heat for you, they do act to cool foods that would otherwise be too hot for a Pitta. These include cumin, saffron, and turmeric, which can be soothing for the Pitta. Below is a list of spices to favor and those to avoid:

Favor	Avoid
● Basil (fresh)	● Ajwan
● Black Pepper (small amounts)	● Allspice
● Cardamom	● Anise
● Cinnamon (small amounts)	● Basil (dry)
● Coriander (seeds or powder)	● Bay Leaf
● Cumin (seeds or powder)	● Caraway
● Dill	● Cayenne
● Fennel	● Cloves
● Ginger (fresh)	● Fenugreek
● Mint	● Garlic
● Neem Leaves	● Ginger (dry)
● Orange Peel	● Hing (Asafoetida)
● Parsley	● Mace
● Peppermint	● Marjoram
● Saffron	● Mustard Seeds
● Spearmint	● Nutmeg
● Tarragon	● Oregano
● Turmeric	● Paprika
● Vanilla	● Pippali
● Wintergreen	● Poppy Seeds
	● Rosemary
	● Sage
	● Salt
	● Savory
	● Thyme
	● Trikatu

Following these food recommendations will help to keep Pitta balanced, particularly in the winter season. In addition to the foods to favor or avoid, here are some specific winter Pitta recipes:

Pitta Winter Recipes

Maple Tapioca

Ingredients:

- 6 to 8 dried apricots, peaches, figs, or prunes (optional)
- 5 tablespoons granulated (quick) tapioca
- 2 ½ cups milk, cow or goat
- ¼ teaspoon sea salt
- 2 eggs
- 1/3 cup maple syrup
- ½ teaspoon vanilla extract
- 1/8 teaspoon cinnamon
- 1/8 teaspoon ground cardamom

Optional Toppings: toasted blanched almonds, slivered, and toasted unsweetened shredded coconut, about 2 tablespoons of each.

Directions:

Chop the dried fruit into ½ inch pieces. Place fruit, tapioca, milk, and salt in the top of a double boiler and cook over boiling water for ten minutes, stirring only if the mixture begins to stick. Add maple syrup. Reduce heat and simmer for 2 minutes on very low heat. In a separate small bowl, beat the eggs. Mix ½ cup of the hot tapioca mixture into the eggs to avoid curdling, then gradually add the egg mixture to the rest of the tapioca, cooking for 3 to 4 minutes more, stirring constantly. Add vanilla and spices, stir well. Remove from heat and cool. Garnish with toasted almonds and coconut as desired. Serve warm or cold.

Hot Spiced Chai

Ingredients:

- 3 cups water
- 4 cloves
- 2 pinches ground nutmeg
- 2 pinches ground cinnamon
- 2 pinches ground cardamom
- ½ inch piece of fresh ginger
- 1 teaspoon black tea (or dandelion root or lemon grass)
- 1 cup milk
- 2 teaspoons sweetener of your choice

Directions:

Boil the water with the spices for 2 minutes. Add the tea and simmer for two minutes. Add the milk and heat until hot, but not boiling. Add sweetener and serve.

Rice Porridge

This is a good breakfast porridge for maintaining balance for both Pitta and Vata. It slightly increases Kapha if you eat a generous amount because it absorbs large quantities of water. Quinoa can be substituted for rice, which is a better choice for the Kapha dosha.

Ingredients:

- 1 cup white basmati rice
- ½ tablespoon ghee
- 1 pinch of cumin seeds
- ¼ teaspoon of salt
- 2 cups of hot water

Directions:

Wash rice thoroughly. Heat the ghee or oil over medium heat and sauté the cumin seeds for a few moments until the aroma starts to come out. Add the rice and mix well. Add the salt and hot water. Bring to a boil and boil for 2–3 minutes. Turn down the heat to very low and cover. For stickier rice, leave the lid ajar. For drier rice keep the lid on tight. Cook until the rice is tender—about 15–20 minutes.

Chapter Summary

In this chapter, we've discussed the Pitta dosha as well as the best foods you can consume to stay balanced, particularly in the winter months. Specifically, we've discussed the following topics:

- Pitta qualities;
- Pitta emotional characteristics;
- Pitta physical characteristics;
- Favorable foods for Pitta in winter;
- Foods to avoid in winter;
- Best foods for the winter months;
- A winter food guideline for the Pitta dosha with recipes.

In the next chapter, we'll discuss Vata nutrition for the winter months.

2

VATA NUTRITION FOR STAYING BALANCED IN WINTER

W inter is the season of Vata, the dosha associated with air. For this reason, this dosha has cold, airy tendencies. Those with Vata as their principle dosha tend to go where the wind blows them. Vata also embodies communication and movement. It is responsible for the information that enters the body and mind. Vata types have active minds, are quick to speak, and often have joints that crack. As the seasons change from summer to fall and then winter, Vatas can feel these changes internally. When their balance is disturbed, a routine of rest and activity can help to re-establish harmony. It's also vital that Vatas follow a consistent diet to avoid restlessness, insomnia, constipation, dry skin, and anxiety. Let's take a closer look at this powerful dosha.

Vata Qualities

This dosha has control over the flow of your thoughts and feelings and your nervous system's activities. It also governs your bodily fluids, and your prana flows. Vata types often suffer from anxiety, and they are sometimes spacey. This is due in part to their energetic, creative minds that capture their attention. When they are well-balanced, a Vata is lively and enthusiastic. That may be due to the dosha's characteristics: being quick and adaptable, always moving, being rough, irregular, dry, light, and cold. Let's look a little more closely at some specific physical and emotional characteristics.

- **Physical Characteristics:** Vatas are typically thin with light frames, and they are highly adaptable. They experience energy in bursts that are followed by fatigue. It's not unusual for a Vata to experience dry skin and cold extremities. Because of their active, creative minds keep them from sleeping soundly, and they usually have a sensitive digestive system. When they're out of balance, Vatas can suffer from weight loss, constipation, arthritis, weakness, restlessness, and generalized aches and pains.
- **Emotional Characteristics:** Vatas love excitement and new experiences, but they are quick to anger. Luckily, they are also quick to forgive. They also tend to be creative, flexible people, and with active minds, they are often the life of the party. They are great

conversationalists. When they are out of balance, Vatas worry a lot and suffer from insomnia and anxiety.

To stay balanced, Vatas should maintain consistent routines that include gentle, regulated exercises. It's also essential for them to nurture themselves in calm, safe, and comforting environments. To soothe and ground Vatas, Ayurvedic massages can help, but it's also crucial for Vata to avoid cold, windy, dry climates. It can also be helpful to minimize travel and to avoid noisy, crowded places. Vatas should also take care to stay warm and maintain a good diet for their dosha.

Staying Balanced in Winter

In winter, since this is Vata's season, you want to counter the Vata qualities of cold, wind, and dryness to stay balanced. That means eating heavier, oilier, and more substantive foods to ground, lubricate, and nourish your system. Let's look at the foods to favor.

Favorable Foods

In general, warm, nourishing foods with a moderately heavy texture that includes butter and fat are suitable for Vata types. Sweet-tasting foods, as well as salty and sour foods, are also soothing. The very best foods include warm milk, cream, butter, warm soups, stews, fresh-baked bread, hot cereals, raw nuts, and nut butter. Hot herbal teas are great for feeding

Vata's energetic mind, as are warm or hot sweet fruits. The best spices include cinnamon, cardamom, cumin, cloves, ginger, and garlic.

For Vata in winter, sweet, sour, and salty tastes and warm, soft, well-cooked foods that are nicely spiced, but not too hot is preferable. You also want to choose sweet, heavy fruits--including avocado--as your body will do well with these. As for vegetables and legumes, you want to favor asparagus, beets, carrots, chilies, green beans, mustard greens, okra, olives, onion, parsnip, sweet potatoes, spinach, summer squash, zucchini, kidney beans, mung beans, tofu, miso, tur dal, and urad dal. It's best to cook them well using generous amounts of oil, which is particularly important so that they won't be as drying. Vata can eat most dairy products during the winter months, but the best choices are hot milk, ghee, and cottage cheese. As a Vata, you can also feel free to eat as much amaranth, cooked oats, quinoa, brown rice, basmati rice, wheat, most meats, nuts and seeds, most oils, and spices as you like in the winter. Most natural sweeteners are acceptable as well, but honey, molasses, and jaggery are particularly beneficial because of their heating qualities.

Acceptable Winter Indulgences

Due to the heaviness of winter and Vata's digestive fire's added strength, you can indulge in certain foods in winter that you might not usually want to consume. These include an occasional bowl of bean soup, caffeinated tea, and coffee or espresso with cream and sugar. Sweet treats can also offer support for your system in the winter.

Foods to Minimize

While Vatas have a robust system, there are some foods they should avoid in winter. These include the following:

- Astringent fruits such as pears, pomegranates, or dried fruits. Apples are okay as long as they are cooked and garnished with ghee.
- Barley, corn, millet, oat bran, dry oats, popcorn, rice cakes or crackers, rye, pork, rabbit, and venison.
- Most beans, other than those listed above.
- White sugar, raw vegetables, iced drinks, and frozen foods like ice cream.
- Vatas should avoid eating leftovers.

Lifestyle Adjustments

The most important thing for Vatas in winter is to establish a routine. If you're a Vata, you want to get up and go to bed at the same general time each day. You should also eat meals at regular intervals and develop some good work and exercise habits. Massages are also beneficial, and you should use sesame oil for those to keep from drying. Regarding exercise, you can push yourself more during this time, but don't overdo it. If yoga is among your exercise options, you'll want to move mindfully and gracefully, and you'll want to use restorative postures. Also, be sure to end your practice with a corpse pose and hold it for a long time. Finally, resist the temptation to overbook your commitments. Get in the rhythm of the season and take it slow and quiet. Winter is an excellent time to replenish lost stores of energy and embrace stillness in your life.

Vata Food Guidelines

The following are basic guidelines for those whose primary dosha is Vata. These recommendations should be useful for maintaining balance or restoring it as necessary.

Fruits

Sweet, nourishing fruits are best for Vata, and most of the time, they should be cooked or stewed to add warmth, moisture, and sweetness. This also makes them easier to digest. Vatas want to avoid those fruits that are too cooling, astringent, or rough. That means they should avoid dried fruits. It's also best to consume fruits without any other food, so allow at least 30 minutes to pass before or after eating something else. This rule does not apply to those kinds of fruits considered to be vegetables like avocados, cucumbers, and tomatoes. The following is a guideline for which fruits to favor and which to avoid.

Favor	Avoid
• Apples (cooked)	• Apples (raw)
• Applesauce	• Bananas (green)
• Apricots	• Cranberries
• Bananas (ripe, not green)	• Dates (dry)
• Berries	• Dried Fruit, in general
• Cantaloupe	• Figs (dry)
• Cherries	• Pears
• Coconut	• Persimmons
• Dates (fresh, cooked or soaked)	• Pomegranate
• Figs (fresh, cooked or soaked)	• Prunes (dry)
• Grapefruit	• Raisins (dry)
• Grapes	• Watermelon
• Kiwi	
• Lemon	
• Lime	
• Mango	
• Melons	
• Oranges	
• Papaya	
• Peaches	
• Pineapple	
• Plums	
• Prunes (cooked or soaked)	
• Raisins (cooked or soaked)	
• Tamarind	

Vegetables

As a Vata, you want to counter the qualities of Vata to stay balanced. Therefore, the best vegetables to consume are those that are sweet, moist, and cooked. Root vegetables such as potatoes are very beneficial since they grow underground, grounding and stabilizing airy Vata. Vata should avoid dry, rough, and cold vegetables, which means raw vegetables. If you do eat some raw vegetables, do so only at midday and in limited quantities. Alternatively, cooking these kinds of vegetables well will offset their dry and rough qualities. Below is a guideline for the vegetables to favor and those to avoid.

Favor	Avoid
● Asparagus	● Artichokes
● Avocado	● Beet Greens
● Beets	● Bell Peppers
● Carrots, Cooked	● Bitter Melon
● Chilies (in very small quantities)	● Broccoli
● Cilantro	● Brussels Sprouts
● Cucumber	● Burdock Root
● Garlic	● Cabbage
● Green Beans	● Carrots, Raw
● Green Chilies	● Cauliflower
● Leeks	● Celery
● Mustard Greens	● Chilies (in excess)
● Okra	● Corn, Fresh
● Olives (black)	● Dandelion Greens
● Onion, Cooked	● Eggplant
● Parsnip	● Jerusalem Artichokes
● Peas, Cooked	● Kale
● Pumpkin	● Kohlrabi
● Rutabaga	● Lettuce
● Spinach, Cooked	● Mushrooms
● Squash, Summer	● Olives, Green
● Squash, Winter	● Onion, Raw
● Sweet Potatoes	● Peas, Raw
● Watercress	● Peppers, Hot
● Zucchini	● Potatoes, White
	● Radishes
	● Spinach, Raw
	● Sprouts
	● Tomatoes
	● Turnips

Grains

Vatas should consume those grains that are sweet, nourishing, easy to digest, and well-cooked like oatmeal, cream of wheat, and rice pudding. These are especially comforting for Vatas. Grains to avoid include light, dry, or rough, as well as dense and heavy. These can cause disturbances for Vatas. Below are guidelines for which grains to favor and which to avoid.

Favor	Avoid
• Amaranth	• Barley
• Durham Flour	• Buckwheat
• Oats, Cooked	• Cereals (cold, dry, or puffed)
• Pancakes	• Corn
• Quinoa	• Couscous
• Rice (all types)	• Crackers
• Seitan	• Granola
• Sprouted Wheat Bread	• Millet
• Wheat	• Muesli
	• Oat Bran
	• Oats, Dry
	• Pasta, Wheat
	• Rice Cakes
	• Rye
	• Spelt
	• Tapioca
	• Wheat Bran
	• Yeasted Bread

Legumes

Vatas can only eat a limited selection of legumes, and they should be well-cooked and well-spiced. Choose from beans that are less dense, rough, and drier than the other legumes, since these cook quickly, are easy to digest, and offer a grounding quality. Below are guidelines for which legumes to favor and which to avoid.

Favor	Avoid
● Lentils, Red	● Adzuki Beans
● Miso	● Black Beans
● Mung Beans	● Black-Eyed Peas
● Mung Dal, Split	● Garbanzo Beans (Chickpeas)
● Soy Cheese	● Kidney Beans
● Soy Milk (served warm)	● Lentils, Brown
● Soy Sauce	● Lima Beans
● Soy Meats	● Navy Beans
● Tofu (served hot)	● Pinto Beans
● Toor Dal	● Soy Beans
● Urad Dal	● Soy Flour
	● Soy Powder
	● Split Peas
	● Tempeh
	● White Beans

Dairy

For the most part, dairy products are balancing for Vatas. Still, it's best to avoid highly processed dairy products like powdered milk or cow's milk. It's better to boil cow's milk, and then, for added sweetness, you can spice it with cinnamon and nutmeg. Cold cow's milk isn't easy for Vatas to digest, so best to serve it hot. It's also preferable to consume dairy products at least an hour before or after consuming other food. If you need milk with your meal, almond and rice milk make handy substitutes. Below are some guidelines for which dairy products to favor and which to avoid.

Favor	Avoid
● Butter	● Frozen Yogurt
● Buttermilk	● Powdered Milk
● Cheese	
● Cottage Cheese	
● Cow's milk	
● Ghee	
● Goat's Milk	
● Ice Cream (in moderation)	
● Sour Cream (in moderation)	
● Yogurt (fresh)	

Nuts and Seeds

All nuts and seeds should be consumed in moderation. They are oily and nutritious, and they also provide a great combination of proteins and healthy fats, which are very beneficial. But, they are also quite heavy and should be consumed only in small quantities. Below are the guidelines for which nuts and seeds to favor and which to avoid.

Favor	Avoid
• Almonds • Brazil Nuts • Cashews • Coconut • Hazelnuts • Macadamia Nuts • Peanuts • Pecans • Pine Nuts • Pistachios • Pumpkin Seeds • Sesame Seeds • Sunflower Seeds • Walnuts	• Popcorn

Meat and Eggs

Eggs and a variety of meats are fine for those Vatas who like them. It's best to choose those meats that are nourishing, sweet, moist, and easy to digest. Meats that are too light and dry or too heavy should be avoided. Below are guidelines for which meats to favor and which to avoid.

Favor	Avoid
● Beef	● Lamb
● Buffalo	● Mutton
● Chicken (especially dark)	● Pork
● Duck	● Rabbit
● Eggs	● Venison
● Fish (fresh and saltwater)	● Turkey (white)
● Salmon	
● Sardines	
● Seafood	
● Shrimp	
● Tuna Fish	
● Turkey (dark)	

Oils

The oils you choose to consume should be organic because toxins concentrate in fats. That said, most oils are beneficial for Vatas as long as they are high in quality. The best choices are sesame oil, almond oil, coconut oil, olive oil, and ghee. The less favorable oils include those that are too light and dry, too difficult to digest, or highly processed. Below are guidelines for which oils to favor and which to avoid.

Favor	Avoid
• Almond Oil	• Canola Oil
• Avocado Oil	• Corn Oil
• Castor Oil	• Flaxseed Oil
• Coconut Oil	• Soy Oil
• Ghee	
• Mustard Oil	
• Olive Oil	
• Peanut Oil	
• Safflower Oil	
• Sesame Oil	
• Sunflower Oil	

Sweeteners

The majority of sweeteners are good for Vatas, but you don't want to consume large quantities of refined sugar. It's better to choose natural types of sweeteners rather than those that are highly processed. Rather than using white sugar, try something like honey or molasses or even use something like dates or other sweet fruits. Below are guidelines for the kinds of sweeteners to favor and those to avoid.

Favor	Avoid
● Barley Malt	● Artificial Sweeteners
● Date Sugar	● White Sugar
● Fructose	● Honey (heated or cooked)
● Fruit Juice Concentrates	
● Honey (raw)	
● Jaggery	
● Maple Syrup (in moderation)	
● Molasses	
● Rice Syrup	
● Sucanat	
● Turbinado	

Spices

Most spices are great for Vatas as long as the dishes you're making aren't too fiery because of cayenne pepper, chili peppers, or something similar. But, mostly, you have the freedom to experiment with a wide variety of exotic spices, and these generally help to fortify the digestive strength of a Vata. Below are guidelines for which spices to favor and which to consume only in moderation.

Favor	Use in Moderation
• Ajwan	• Cayenne Pepper
• Allspice	• Chili Powder
• Anise	• Fenugreek
• Basil	• Horseradish
• Bay Leaf	• Neem Le
• Black Pepper	
• Caraway	
• Cardamom	
• Cinnamon	
• Cloves	
• Coriander (seeds or powder)	
• Cumin (seeds or powder)	
• Dill	
• Fennel	
• Garlic	
• Ginger (fresh or dried)	
• Hing (Asafoetida)	
• Mace	
• Marjoram	
• Mint	
• Mustard Seeds	
• Nutmeg	
• Oregano	
• Paprika	
• Parsley	
• Peppermint	
• Pippali	
• Poppy Seeds	
• Rosemary	
• Saffron	
• Salt	
• Savory	
• Tarragon	
• Thyme	
• Turmeric	
• Vanilla	

In addition to the general guidelines for the foods to avoid and favor as a Vata, here are a few specific recipes to try:

Vata Balancing Recipes

Winter Pasta for Vata

Ingredients:

Serves 4

- 1 pound (500 g) fresh linguine, fettuccine, or spaghetti or ½ pound (230 g) dried
- ⅓ cup (80 ml) oil
- Pinch of hing (optional)
- 2 cups (180 g) carrots, cut into 2-inch (5 cm) lengths and finely julienned
- 3 cups (330 g) fennel stalks, cut into 2-inch (5 cm) lengths and slivered lengthwise
- Up to 4 tablespoons chopped fennel tops (if on the fennel bulb)
- Liquid seasoning or salt
- 1 tablespoon fennel seeds
- 2 tablespoons lemon juice
- ½ cup (50 g) slivered pecans, lightly toasted
- Black pepper

Directions:

1. Cook the pasta until it's al dente. Drain.
2. Heat the oil in a large skillet over low heat. Add the hing and sauté for 30 seconds until fragrant. Add the carrots, fennel, fennel tops, and sprinkle with liquid seasoning or salt. Cover and cook until tender, stirring occasionally.
3. Toss the vegetables, fennel seeds, lemon juice, Ginger Gremolata, pecans, and a sprinkling of black pepper with the pasta. Adjust the seasoning. Serve with Ginger Gremolata

Ginger Gremolata

Ingredients:

- 1 tablespoon minced fresh ginger
- 1 tablespoon finely-grated lemon zest
- 1 cup (240 ml) minced flat-leaf parsley

Directions:

Mix all the ingredients together.

Steamed Sesame Greens

Ingredients:

Serves 2 - 4

- 1 tbsp ghee
- 1-inch fresh ginger, peeled & grated
- 1/4 tsp whole mustard seeds
- ½ tsp coriander seeds
- 4-5 leaves kale, ends trimmed, leaves roughly chopped
- 4-5 leaves chard, ends trimmed, leaves roughly chopped
- 1 tsp white sesame seeds
- Juice of ½ lemon

Directions:

1. Place a large, heavy-bottomed skillet on the stovetop and add the ghee. Cook over medium-low heat until the ghee is completely melted.
2. Add the fresh ginger, mustard seeds, coriander seeds, and toast for one minute, stirring frequently to prevent any sticking or burning.
3. Add the kale and chard, stirring until tender. Avoid over cooking, you want the greens to remain bright and vibrant. Remove the skillet from the stovetop. Finish with a squeeze of fresh lemon juice and toss with the sesame seeds. Serve right away while the greens are hot.
4. To assemble: Layer with sautéed greens and roasted pumpkin. Drizzle with miso tahini sauce. Garnish each

bowl with a handful of sunflower and cilantro microgreens, or fresh sprouts of your choice.

Chapter Summary

In this chapter, we discussed the Vata dosha and what foods are best to maintain balance, especially in the winter.

- The characteristics of Vata;
- The physical characteristics;
- The emotional characteristics;
- Favorable foods for Vata in winter;
- Foods to avoid or reduce for Vata in winter;
- Best foods for winter and a few specific recipes.

In the next chapter, we'll discuss the Kapha dosha.

3

KAPHA NUTRITION FOR STAYING BALANCED IN WINTER

K apha is the dosha that embodies love and structure. It's associated season is spring. It is responsible for your body's moisture, stability, and energy storage. It's related to water and earth elements, which help keep the body's structure together as it supports growth and development. Those whose primary dosha is Kapha are full of love and compassion, and they are very dependable people. Kapha's nature is balanced by light, dry, mobile, and subtle qualities typically found in the autumn. Still, in the winter, the primary attributes present are earth and water, which can aggravate Kapha. If Kapha is your primary dosha, winter can make you more prone to chesty, mucus coughs and colds, and you may also have problems with slow digestion, chills, and swollen joints.

Kapha Qualities

Kaphas tend to be heavier than other types, with bodies that readily store fluids. Temperamentally, they are calm and well-attached, and they frequently dream about water. Let's look at some more specific characteristics:

- **Physical Characteristics:** Kaphas often have very melodic voices, strong physical builds, and excellent stamina. Moreover, they usually have smooth, radiant skin, regular digestive patterns, and sleep soundly. However, those Kaphas who indulge in excess often quickly gain weight, retain fluids, and have allergies. An unbalanced Kapha may be obese, sleep excessively, be lethargic, and have asthma, diabetes, and depression.

- **Emotional Characteristics:** Kapha types are calm, loving, and thoughtful people who enjoy life and are very comfortable in their routines. They are typically loyal, patient, healthy, and supportive people who love reading, music, and relaxing. However, when unbalanced, they often will cling to things even though they no longer serve a constructive purpose in their lives. Additionally, unbalanced Kaphas can be stubborn and resist change.

Staying balanced means rising before dawn, sleeping less, and refraining from naps during the day. Plenty of exercises with stimulating activities to energize the body and mind and increase the metabolic rate are significant for Kapha. It's also essential to have exciting things in your life so that you can break away from stagnation and the tendency of Kapha types to cling to old ways of acting and thinking. In that way, welcoming change helps keep you balanced. It's also helpful to stay warm and follow a good diet.

Favorable Foods

In general, Kaphas in winter should eat warm, light, and dry foods that are lightly cooked. If this is your type, you can also feel free to eat raw fruits and vegetables and spicy foods such as Mexican or Indian food. These are incredibly helpful for the winter months. It's also a good idea for Kaphas to use dry cooking methods like baking, grilling, broiling, or sauteing rather than steaming, boiling, or poaching. These are general guidelines, but let's look at some specific tips for the wintertime.

Staying Balanced in Winter

Dietary tips:

- Warm porridge with cinnamon, cloves, and honey make a great breakfast.
- For lunch and dinner, avoid cold, wet, and damp foods taken straight from the refrigerator. You also want to avoid those foods that are excessively sweet.
- Drink warm, spicy drinks throughout the day.

- In the evening, a warming glass of wine can help encourage circulation and stimulate digestion.
- Another good evening drink is a glass of hot, spicy milk with herbs like cinnamon and nutmeg.

Lifestyles Tips:

- Kaphas can sleep a little later in the wintertime since staying warm in bed helps with rejuvenation.
- Upon arising, it can help to use stimulating oils like cinnamon and clove when you brush your teeth. It's also good to wash your mouth out with warm water instead of cold water to clear your congestion.
- Kaphas should practice self-massage a few times each week using warming oils like sesame oil to help offset the coldness. It will also help with achy joints. Be sure to allow the oil to absorb before taking a warm shower and use an exfoliator to stimulate blood flow on chilly mornings.
- Your first drink of the day should be something warm and invigorating like ginger, turmeric, cinnamon, or clove tea. Add a twist of lemon and some honey to wake up your appetite and stimulate a healthy bowel movement.
- For your yoga practice, stimulating postures like sun salutations will help you feel warm and energized.

Backward and forward bends will help open the chest and get areas of stagnation moving.

- Ginger, elderberry, and echinacea tea in the morning can help keep colds and coughs at bay.
- It's also good to include warm, mildly spiced, and slightly salty foods in your winter diet, helping keep the digestive fires healthy and reduce excess Kapha.

The most critical thing Kaphas can do as autumn transitions into winter is to allow your body and mind time to adjust to the new environmental changes. Give it time and support with adequate rest and sleep periods, a nutritious diet, regular exercise, and a positive state of mind. This will allow your body to recharge and feel ready for the long, cold months ahead. The following presents a list of foods for Kapha to both favor and avoid.

Kapha Winter Nutrition Guidelines

Fruits

The best fruits for Kapha include those that are astringent and only slightly sweet. Dried fruits are okay, but only in small quantities since they are so dense. Exceptionally sweet or sour fruits and those that are heavy, dense, or watery should be avoided. Additionally, fruits should be eaten alone, so allow at least 30 minutes before eating other foods. That rule doesn't apply to those fruits we call vegetables like avocados, cucumbers, or tomatoes. Below are the guidelines for fruit.

Favor	Avoid
• Apples	• Bananas
• Applesauce	• Cantaloupe
• Apricots	• Coconut
• Berries	• Dates
• Cherries	• Figs (fresh)
• Cranberries	• Grapes (green)
• Figs (dry)	• Grapefruit
• Grapes (red, purple, black)	• Kiwi
• Lemons	• Melons
• Limes	• Oranges
• Mango	• Papaya
• Peaches	• Pineapple
• Pears	• Plums
• Persimmons	• Rhubarb
• Pomegranates	• Tamarin
• Prunes	• Watermelon
• Raisins	
• Raspberries	
• Strawberries	

Vegetables

The best vegetables for Kapha are those that are pungent, bitter, and astringent. Cooked vegetables are more comfortable to digest, and therefore, raw vegetables should be consumed in small quantities only and at midday when your digestion is most efficient. Raw vegetables are better in the spring or summer for Kapha than in the fall and winter. Kaphas should also avoid those vegetables which are heavy, dense, oily, or watery. Below are the general guidelines for which vegetables to favor and which to avoid.

Favor	Avoid
• Artichoke	• Avocado
• Asparagus	• Cucumber
• Beet Greens	• Olives
• Beets	• Parsnips
• Bell Peppers	• Pumpkin
• Bitter Melon	• Squash, Summer
• Broccoli	• Sweet Potatoes
• Brussels Sprouts	• Tomatoes (raw)
• Burdock Root	• Zucchini
• Cabbage	
• Carrots	
• Cauliflower	
• Celery	
• Chilies	
• Cilantro	
• Collard Greens	
• Corn	
• Daikon Radish	
• Dandelion Greens	
• Eggplant	
• Garlic	
• Green Beans	
• Horseradish	
• Jerusalem Artichokes	
• Kale	
• Kohlrabi	
• Leafy Greens	
• Leeks	
• Lettuce	
• Mustard Greens	
• Okra	
• Onions	
• Peas	
• Peppers, Sweet & Hot	
• Potatoes, White	
• Radishes	
• Rutabaga	
• Spaghetti Squash	
• Spinach	
• Sprouts	
• Squash, Winter	
• Tomatoes (cooked)	
• Turnips	
• Watercress	
• Wheat Grass	

Grains

The best grains for Kapha are light, dry, and rough; however, the heavy, nourishing features of grains that make them a staple in our diets are precisely the qualities Kapha wants to avoid. For their benefit, then, Kaphas should reduce their grain consumption overall, but particularly in the case of those grains which are heavy, moist, or dense such as wheat, flours, bread, cooked oats, and pasta. Even the appropriate grains should be eaten in small quantities, and it's a good idea to supplement them with extra legumes or vegetables. Below are guidelines for which grains to favor and which to avoid.

Favor	Avoid
• Amaranth	• Oats (cooked)
• Barley	• Pancakes
• Buckwheat	• Pasta
• Cereal (unsweetened, cold, dry)	• Rice (brown, white)
• Corn	• Wheat
• Couscous	• Yeasted Bread
• Crackers	
• Durham Flour	
• Granola	
• Millet	
• Muesli	
• Oat Bran	
• Oats (dry)	
• Polenta	
• Quinoa	
• Rice (basmati, wild)	
• Rice Cakes	
• Rye	
• Seitan	
• Spelt	
• Sprouted Wheat Bread	
• Tapioca	
• Wheat Bran	

Legumes

Kaphas can enjoy a wide variety of legumes because they are mostly astringent in taste. They should, however, be well-cooked and well-spiced to make them more easily digestible. The only beans Kapha should take care to avoid being too heavy or oily to balance the dosha. Below are the guidelines for which legumes to favor and which to avoid.

Favor	Avoid
• Adzuki Beans • Black Beans • Black-Eyed Peas • Garbanzo Beans (Chickpeas) • Lentils • Lima Beans • Mung Beans • Mung Dal • Navy Beans • Pinto Beans • Split Peas • Soy Milk • Soy Meats • Tempeh • Tofu (served hot) • Toor Dal • White Beans	• Kidney Beans • Miso • Soy Beans • Soy Cheese • Soy Flour • Soy Powder • Soy Sauce • Tofu (served cold) • Urad Dal

Dairy

Diary generally increases mucus production and is heavy, making it something Kapha types should avoid. When you consume dairy products, it should be at least one hour before or after consuming other foods. For Kapha, milk is best boiled and served hot with turmeric or ginger to make it more digestible and less congesting. You should also choose goat's milk since it is lighter, but even this should be consumed in moderation. For milk, almond or rice milk make great substitutes. Below are guidelines for which dairy products to favor and which to avoid.

Favor	Avoid
• Buttermilk • Cottage Cheese (ideally from skim goat's milk) • Ghee • Goat's Cheese (unsalted, not aged) • Goat's Milk (skim) • Yogurt (fresh and diluted)	• Butter • Cheese • Cow's Milk • Frozen Yogurt • Ice Cream • Sour Cream • Yogurt (store-bought)

Nuts and Seeds

Kapha should take care of nuts and seeds since they are heavy, dense, and oily; however, a few types can be consumed in small quantities. Still, they are best enjoyed only once in a while. Below are guidelines for which nuts and seeds to favor and which to avoid.

Favor	Avoid
• Almonds (soaked and peeled) • Charole Nuts • Chia Seeds • Flax Seeds • Popcorn (without salt or butter) • Pumpkin Seeds • Sunflower Seeds	• Brazil Nuts • Cashews • Coconut • Filberts • Macadamia Nuts • Peanuts • Pecans • Pine Nuts • Pistachios • Sesame Seeds • Tahini • Walnuts

Meat and Eggs

Kaphas should consume only those animal foods that are light and relatively dry, like chicken and fish. In general, less meat is better for all doshas, and Kapha can be satisfied easily without meat. Below are guidelines for which meats to favor and which to avoid.

Favor	Avoid
• Chicken (white)	• Beef
• Eggs (not fried, and in moderation)	• Buffalo
• Fish (freshwater)	• Chicken (dark)
• Rabbit	• Duck
• Shrimp	• Fish (saltwater)
• Turkey (white)	• Lamb
• Venison	• Pork
	• Salmon
	• Sardines
	• Seafood
	• Tuna Fish
	• Turkey (dark)

Oils

Oils are mostly too heavy for Kapha, but some are acceptable in small quantities if they are high in quality. Organic oils are better since toxins concentrate in fats. For Kaphas, food can be sauteed in water instead of oil, or it can be steamed. When the oil is necessary, corn oil, sunflower oil, or ghee are best. Below are guidelines for which oils to favor and which to avoid.

Favor	Avoid
• Almond Oil • Corn Oil • Flaxseed Oil • Ghee • Sunflower Oil	• Avocado Oil • Apricot Oil • Coconut Oil • Olive Oil • Primrose Oil • Safflower Oil • Sesame Oil • Soy Oil • Walnut Oil

Sweeteners

In general, sweet tastes don't help Kapha types, and so it is best to avoid them. Honey is one exception because of its dry, light, and has heating qualities, but it should be used only in small quantities. It's particularly helpful since it helps remove toxins from tissues, but heating honey will create toxins, which should be avoided. Additionally, you should only use raw, unprocessed honey. Refined sugars or corn syrup should be avoided altogether. Below are the guidelines for which sweeteners to favor and which to avoid.

Favor	Avoid
• Fruit Juice Concentrates • Honey (raw and unprocessed)	• Artificial Sweeteners • Barley Malt • Date Sugar • Fructose • Honey (cooked, heated or processed) • Jaggery • Maple Syrup • Molasses • Rice Syrup • Sucanat • Turbinado • White Sugar

Spices

Spices are great for Kaphas, so feel free to sample a wide variety of exotic spices. Kapha can handle fiery hot foods, and spices improve the strength of your digestive fire and your overall metabolism. Onions, garlic, ginger, black pepper, chili pepper, and cayenne pepper are incredibly helpful for balancing Kapha. Below are guidelines for which spices to favor and which to avoid.

Favor	Avoid
• Ajwan	• None!
• Allspice	
• Anise	
• Basil	
• Bay Leaf	
• Black Pepper	
• Caraway	
• Cardamom	
• Cayenne	
• Cinnamon	
• Cloves	
• Coriander (seeds or powder)	
• Cumin (seeds or powder)	
• Dill	
• Fennel	
• Fenugreek	
• Garlic	
• Ginger (fresh or dried)	
• Hing (Asafoetida)	
• Mace	
• Marjoram	
• Mint	
• Mustard Seeds	
• Neem Leaves	
• Nutmeg	
• Oregano	
• Paprika	
• Parsley	
• Peppermint	
• Pippali	
• Poppy Seeds	
• Rosemary	
• Saffron	
• Savory	
• Spearmint	
• Tarragon	
• Thyme	
• Trikatu	
• Turmeric	
• Vanilla	
• Wintergreen	

Here are a few recipes for Kapha in the winter season:

Spicy Soup

- 2tsp coriander seeds,
- 2tsp cumin seeds,
- 2 tsp tamarind paste,
- 20 curry leaves,
- 5-6 garlic cloves,
- 10-12 slices fresh ginger,
- a little salt

Directions

Grind into a paste, add 1 liter of water and boil for 20 mins.

Feel free to add if desired:

- Soaked, sprouted and boiled chickpeas. Soaking and sprouting improves their digestibility and are particularly balancing for Kapha due to their astringent (dry) qualities. Carrots, onions or leeks, and spring greens are also a great choice for Kapha.
- Sauté the vegetables in a little oil, then add the cooked chickpeas and spicy soup.
- Simmer for 5-10 mins before serving.

Kapha Pacifying Tea

Ingredients:

- 2 cups water
- 4 teaspoons fresh grated ginger
- ½ teaspoon ashwagandha powder
- 2 teaspoons tulsi powder
- ¼ teaspoon cardamom powder
- ½ lemon squeezed
- Honey to taste

Directions:

Heat the water in a pot over the stove. Mix in the ginger, ashwagandha, tulsi, and cardamom and let the tea come to a rolling boil. Take it off the stove and let it cool down a little. Mix in the fresh lemon juice and just a touch of honey for taste.

Carrot-Squash-White Potato Soup

Ingredients:

Serves 4 to 6

- 8 cups purified water
- 1 pound organic carrots
- 1 pound butternut squash, or any winter squash variety
- 1 large white potato

- 2 teaspoons high-quality, mineral-rich salt such as Celtic sea salt or Himalayan salt
- 3 dried bay leaves
- 1 tablespoon ghee or coconut oil
- ½ bunch of green onions, roughly chopped (use the whole stalk)
- 2 cloves garlic, minced
- 1-inch fresh ginger root, washed and minced
- 1 teaspoon ground nutmeg
- 1 teaspoon cinnamon
- 1 teaspoon dried parsley, basil, or tarragon
- 1 tablespoon miso paste (any variety)
- Dash of apple cider vinegar or fresh lemon juice

Directions:

1. In a large stock pot, bring the water to a boil. Chop the carrots, squash, and white potato into 2-inch chunks. Add them to the water along with the salt and bay leaves. Cover. If you use butternut squash, it's fine to leave the skin on. For other winter squashes, you may want to peel them first, before adding them to the boiling water.

2. Allow it to cook over medium-high heat for about 20 minutes or until you can easily pierce the vegetables with a fork.

3. Meanwhile, in a separate medium-sized saucepan,

sauté the green onions, garlic, and ginger in ghee or coconut oil over medium heat for 3 to 4 minutes, or until the onions are soft and translucent. Add this mixture to the soup. Remove the soup from heat, remove the bay leaves, and add all the remaining ingredients.

4. Puree the soup in a food processor or high-powered blender and serve hot.

Chapter Summary

In this chapter, we have discussed the qualities and nutritional needs for Kapha individuals, particularly in the winter. Specifically, we've covered the following topics:

- Kapha traits;
- Physical characteristics;
- Emotional characteristics;
- Favorable foods for Kapha in winter;
- Foods to avoid for Kapha in winter;
- Foods that are best in the winter with specific recipes.

In the next chapter, we'll examine the best healing practices for each dosha in the winter.

4

PITTA SELF-HEALING PRACTICES IN WINTER

For Pitta, winter can bring a natural balance to your fiery nature, but that doesn't mean you can't suffer from imbalances. How do you know? Well, Pitta types with imbalances often have problems related to excessive heat. That might mean acidity in the mind, or it might manifest in your body as acid indigestion, diarrhea, fever, hot flashes, infections, and rashes. That's not pleasant, so how can you balance it? Let's take a look at some specific things you can do to stay balanced in winter.

Dietary Tips

In general, Pitta needs a lighter, more cooling diet than what might satisfy other people in winter. Follow the specific nutritional guidelines offered in Chapter One, but here are a few other tips:

- Favor ghee, coconut oil, or olive oil for cooking.
- Favor cooling spices like fennel, coriander, cardamom, and turmeric.
- Drink cold, but not ice-cold beverages.
- Avoid spicy foods like chili peppers.
- Avoid vinegar, caffeinated beverages, and chocolate.
- Drink milk boiled with a little ghee, saffron, cardamom, and sugar before going to bed.

It's also a good idea for Pittas to carefully prepare their food and take time to eat a healthy lunch. In addition to dietary tips, there are specific lifestyle recommendations.

Lifestyle Recommendations

The following are lifestyles tips for balancing Pitta in winter:

- Be light-hearted—don't take yourself too seriously.
- Play, particularly with children. It will set your spirit free.
- Don't strain your eyes with a computer or TV, particularly in the evening.
- Exercise, but avoid becoming overheated or embroiled in competitive sports. Walking in nature, especially next to water or in the shade of trees, yoga, swimming, skiing, cycling, etc., are all better exercise choices.
- Protect yourself from the midday sun.
- Retire before 10 PM.

• Practice meditation.

Yoga Poses for Balancing Pitta

The best asanas for Pitta's fiery nature are those that are calming and not overly heating. Pitta's intense, assertive nature requires more calming poses to balance it, which can not only maintain balance in your doshas, but it can help treat conditions like ulcers, hyperacidity, liver disease, and acne. Some of the best yoga poses include those that put pressure on the naval and solar plexus region, and energetically, twisting, folding poses provide a challenge while simultaneously relaxing the body and mind. Here are some great poses to add to your winter line up:

1. Parivrtta Utthita Hasta Padangusthasana-- revolved extended hand to big toe pose

Stand in mountain pose with your feet together and your hands in prayer pose. Shift your weight to your left foot and spread your toes. Lift your right knee to the height of your hip. Keep it bent and hold it with your left hand. Twist your torso to your right and extend your right arm. Guide your bent right leg across your body with your left hand or straighten your right leg and hold your right big toe with your left hand. Relax your shoulders and your jaw. Hold this pose for 3 - 6 breaths before untwisting slowly and returning to standing. Repeat on the other side.

2.Parivrtta Prasarita Padottanasana--revolved wide-legged standing forward bend.

Stand with your feet parallel, about one leg's length apart. On the inhale, raise your arms above your head, and on the exhale, bend forward, folding at the hips. Place your left hand on the floor between your feet and in line with your sternum. Twist your torso to the right and extend your right arm toward the sky. Direct your breath to your waistline and hold this pose for 3 - 6 breaths before unwinding gradually. Repeat the pose on the other side.

3. Sucirandhrasana--eye of the needle pose

Lie on your back and bend both knees. Stack your right ankle on top of your left thigh and flex both feet. With your left hand, hold your right ankle while extending your right arm on the floor at shoulder height. Lower your right foot and left outer leg to the floor while gently twisting to the left. Turn your head to the left, close your eyes, and relax your shoulders. If you wish to increase the stretch in your left hip flexors, use your right leg to gently press your left knee away from your torso. Inhale into the left side of your torso, and on the exhale, relax as you lengthen in the pose. Hold the pose for 3 - 6 breaths before gently unwinding. Repeat on the other side.

By incorporating these activities into your winter routine, Pitta can stay balanced until spring.

Chapter Summary

In this chapter, we've discussed some healing practices for Pittas in the winter. Specifically, we've covered the following topics:

- Signs of too much heat;
- Dietary tips;
- Lifestyle adjustments for staying balanced;
- Yoga poses for reducing heat.

In the next chapter, you will discover the healing techniques for Vata in the winter season.

5

VATA SELF-HEALING PRACTICES IN WINTER

The cooler, drier air of winter can aggravate those with a Vata constitution because air is the dominant element in this dosha. When Vata is balanced, your body moves comfortably, your breathing is regular, your appetite is constant, and you have normal bowel functions. Your attitude is positive, and you're enthusiastic with a healthy desire, good energy, a calm mind, and inspired creativity. When Vata is imbalanced, you might find yourself losing weight, having dry skin and hair, irregular bowel movements, feeling dehydrated, bloating, and suffering from insomnia and anxiety. To avoid imbalance, it's essential to increase the opposing qualities for the Vata dosha.

You'll want to introduce more warmth, earthiness, and oily nourishment to your life to balance Vata. It's crucial to stay warm, keep regular sleep patterns, and consume earthy spices and foods. Vata's diet is about nourishing the nervous system, raising digestive fire, and helping your body absorb nutrients. Stick with the dietary recommendations in Chapter Two, but the following presents a few other nutritional tips and some lifestyle tips for staying balanced in winter.

Dietary Tips

Aside from the earlier chapter's dietary tips, incorporate the following tips into your routine to stay balanced:

- Stick to a consistent pattern of eating--don't overeat or forget to eat. Also, relax and take your time eating.
- Emphasize warm, soupy, heavy, and oily foods and increase your intake of natural oils such as those used in cooking and those found in nut milk, for example.
- Favor sweet, sour, or salty foods as these increase heat and moisture.
- Reduce foods that are cold or dry or very spicy. The latter can upset Vata's sensitive digestion.
- Avoid refined foods, stimulants, and processed foods since they take more energy to break down and use up your heat reserves.
- Consume herbs that support the nervous system, such as ashwagandha and turmeric.
- Take immune-strengthening herbs like elderberry, ginger, and medicinal mushrooms to help prevent lingering colds and flu.

Lifestyle Tips

Aside from being careful with your diet, Vata types want to practice some lifestyle activities to stay balanced:

- Practice daily relaxation methods, such as mindfulness meditation.
- Stay moisturized with warming oil massages using sesame oil, for example.
- Before bed, drink a glass of hot, spicy milk with herbs like cinnamon and nutmeg.
- Practice yoga postures suited to Vata types.

Yoga Poses to Balance Vata in Winter

These poses are particularly helpful for balancing Vata during the cold winter months.

1. Utthita Trikonasana--triangle pose

Stand at the front of your mat, and on the inhale, step back with your left leg. Point your right foot forward and keep your right leg straight. Angle your left foot slightly and shift your hips back as you reach your torso forward. Draw your tailbone back as you lengthen your spine and spiral your right hand down to the mat as your left hand reaches up to the sky. With your right palm on the mat and left hand skyward, breathe into the pose and hold for 3 - 6 breaths. Raise back up and step back to the front of the mat. Repeat on the other side.

2. Vrksasana--tree pose

Begin standing at the front of your mat with your feet together. Spread your toes wide and shift your weight to your left foot. Draw your right foot upward and place your foot flat on your thigh above or below (but not on) the left knee. Direct your bent right knee out to the side of your body. Draw your tailbone down as you square and level your hips forward. Bring your hands to the heart center, and on the inhale, reach your hands skyward as you draw your shoulder blades together and down your back. Keep your gaze facing forward. Hold this pose for 3 - 6 breaths before sliding your foot back down to the mat in a controlled manner. Repeat on the other side.

3. Salamba Shirshasana--headstand

Begin on your knees and place your head flat on the mat. Clasp your hands around your head and place your elbows on the mat on either side of your head. Stack your hips over your shoulders and engage your core as you raise your straight legs above your body. Your body should be in a straight line from your head to your toes. You may do this pose against a wall to help you get into the pose until you can do it without assistance. Keep your gaze forward and hold this pose for 5 - 10 minutes. When you're ready to end the pose, bring your legs down to the mat in a controlled manner.

These activities will help you keep Vata balanced in the winter.

Chapter Summary

In this chapter, we've reviewed several lifestyle changes to balance Vata in the winter season. Specifically, we've discussed the following topics:

- Recognizing imbalances in Vata during the winter;
- Dietary tips for balancing Vata in winter;
- Lifestyle choices for Vata in winter;
- The importance of establishing routines;
- Yoga poses for balancing Vata.

In the next chapter, you will discover how to balance Kapha in the winter season.

6

KAPHA SELF-HEALING PRACTICES IN WINTER

K apha is the dosha associated with springtime, and the problem for these types in winter is that they can allow themselves to become too sedentary. That can result in several adverse effects, including weight gain, depression, lethargy, poor circulation, respiratory problems, and oily skin. As with the other doshas, you want to follow the dietary guidelines presented in Chapter Three, but there are a few other tips for staying balanced presented here.

Dietary Tips

Follow the recommendations presented in the earlier chapter, but here are a few other tips:

- Use warming spices like ginger, turmeric, black pepper, cayenne peppers, and chili peppers.

- Avoid heavy, overly oily, salty, or deep-fried foods.
- Consume stews, warm grains, lentils, and beans with a lot of ghee.
- Drink lots of warming drinks.

Lifestyle Tips

Aside from the dietary tips, these lifestyle tips can help Kaphas stay balanced through the long winter months:

- Take hot showers and visit the sauna.
- Dry brush your skin and give yourself a daily oil massage. Dry brushing and massage help detoxify the skin and improve circulation.
- Wear warm, colorful clothing with shades of bright red, orange, and yellow. This inspires warmth and a positive mood throughout the long winter.
- Practice invigorating yoga like Ashtanga or Vinyasa yoga.
- Take an invigorating walk outside in nature.

Yoga Poses to Balance Kapha in Winter

The following yoga poses are perfect for balancing Kapha.

1. Dhanurasana--bow pose

Lie flat on your stomach, keep your chin on the mat with your hands at your sides, palms up. On the exhale, bend your knees and bring your heels as close as possible to your butt. Your knees should be hip-width apart. Lift your hands and grab your ankles. Wrap your fingers around your ankle. Keep your toes pointed. On the inhale, lift your heels away from your butt as you keep a hold on your ankles. At the same time, lift your head, chest, and thighs off the mat, rotating your shoulders as you do. Your core should be the only part of your body touching the mat. Draw your tailbone into the mat to deepen into the stretch. Look straight ahead and hold the pose for approximately 15 seconds as you focus on your breathing. Exhale and release the pose. Relax for a few seconds and repeat the pose. Do this three times.

2. Virabhadrasana--warrior I pose

Begin in mountain pose and step your left foot back with the toes pointing slightly out and your feet hip-distance apart. Adjust your stance as necessary to feel stable and grounded through your feet. Bring your hands to your hips and align them with the mat's front edge by rolling your outer right hip back a bit and the outer left hip forward. Keep your upper body facing the front edge of the mat and your shoulders level. Bend your right knee until the right thigh is parallel to the floor. Keep your weight on your front heel and big toe. Press your back down and lift your inner arch. Make sure the back leg stays engaged as this is your anchor. Lengthen your spine and spread your collarbones as you lift your arms overhead and open your chest. Widen between the shoulder blades and firm your triceps to straighten the arms. Stay in this pose for 5 - 15 breaths. To come out of the pose, inhale as you straighten your front leg. Exhale and bring your arms down before stepping your back foot forward. Repeat on the other side.

3. Virabhadrasana II--warrior II pose

Begin in mountain pose and step back with your left leg, toes slightly pointing in. Press the four corners of your feet down and firm your legs. On the inhale, raise your arms parallel to the floor, keep your shoulders down and your neck long. As you exhale, bend your right knee, but keep it over the ankle. Adjust the position of your feet to find stability in the pose. Roll the top of your thigh down towards the floor on the right and press down through your big toe to balance. Press the top of your left thigh back and ground the outside of your left foot into the floor. Lengthen your spine as you extend through your collar-bones and fingertips. Direct your gaze out over your right hand. Stay in this pose for 5 breaths before pressing your feet and straightening your legs on the inhale. Switch the orientation of your feet and repeat on the other side.

Practicing these poses daily will help Kapha stay balanced.

Chapter Summary

In this chapter, we discussed the best way for Kaphas to stay balanced in the winter. Specifically, the following topics:

- The nature of Kaphas in the winter;
- Dietary tips to stay balanced for Kapha in winter;
- Lifestyle changes to add to your routine;
- The best yoga poses for Kapha to stay balanced.

In the next section, I'll present a few final thoughts.

FINAL WORDS

It should come as no surprise that our bodies go through changes following seasonal changes. Your body ebbs and flows just like everything else in nature. To maintain health, it's essential to recognize these changes and make adjustments to balance your doshas, particularly your primary dosha.

Doshas are your life forces, and every individual has a unique mix of the three life forces: Pitta, Vata, and Kapha. Keeping these doshas balanced throughout the year will help you achieve optimal health and energy for managing your busy life. To balance these doshas, you want to make dietary and lifestyle adjustments appropriate for the time of year and your primary dosha. Making these adjustments will increase your energy, boost your immune system, and help keep you physically, emotionally, mentally, and spiritually happy and healthy.

These books are designed to instruct you in the best practices for balancing your doshas in each of the four seasons. This book has presented information for keeping your doshas balanced in the wintertime. It's crucial to pay attention to this time of year and make the necessary adjustments to stay properly balanced. Should you encounter imbalances, the techniques and dietary guidelines presented in this book can help you to reestablish harmony. My sincere wish is that you live well and enjoy contentment, harmony, and optimal health using these practices.

Be sure to check out www.pureture.com for my other books that take an alternative and holistic approach to health and wellness. You will also find the other seasonal books for the Ayurveda Wellness 101 series.

If you found this book helpful and insightful, then I'd love to hear from you and about your experience. You are more than welcome to email me personally at pureture@pureture.com where I do actually read everyone's emails and I do respond because I'm not a robot. I love hearing from my readers and getting to know each of you.

Cheers to healthy health!

~Pureture, HHP

REFERENCES

Ayurvedic Herbal Medicine. (n.d.). *Spring Recipes To Reduce Vata | Ayush Herbs | Ayurvedic Herbal Medicine.* Retrieved September 8, 2020, from https://www.ayush.com/spring-recipes-to-reduce-vata

Banyan Botanicals. (2019a, June 3). *Pitta-Pacifying Diet.* https://www.banyanbotanicals.com/info/ayurvedic-living/living-ayurveda/diet/pitta-pacifying-diet/

Banyan Botanicals. (2019b, June 5). *Pitta-Pacifying Yoga.* https://www.banyanbotanicals.com/info/ayurvedic-living/living-ayurveda/yoga/pitta-pacifying-yoga/

Banyan Botanicals. (2020a, February 17). *Spring for Pitta.* https://www.banyanbotanicals.com/info/ayurvedic-living/living-ayurveda/seasonal-guides/spring-guide/spring-guide-pitta/

Banyan Botanicals. (2020b, February 17). *Spring for Vata.* https://www.banyanbotanicals.com/info/ayurvedic-living/living-ayurveda/seasonal-guides/spring-guide/spring-guide-vata/

Banyan Botanicals. (2020c, February 19). *Spring for Kapha.* https://www.banyanbotanicals.com/info/ayurvedic-living/living-ayurveda/seasonal-guides/spring-guide/spring-guide-kapha/

Banyan Botanicals. (2020d, March 25). *Spring Rejuvenation for Kapha.* https://www.banyanbotanicals.com/info/ayurvedic-living/living-ayurveda/rejuvenation/spring-rejuvenation-guide/spring-rejuvenation-guide-kapha/

Banyan Botanicals. (2020e, March 25). *Spring Rejuvenation for Pitta.* https://www.banyanbotanicals.com/info/ayurvedic-living/living-ayurveda/rejuvenation/spring-rejuvenation-guide/spring-rejuvenation-guide-pitta/

Banyan Botanicals. (2020f, March 25). *Spring Rejuvenation for Vata.* https://www.banyanbotanicals.com/info/ayurvedic-living/living-ayurveda/rejuvenation/spring-rejuvenation-guide/spring-rejuvenation-guide-vata/

Blossom, S. (2018, September 26). *Rice Porridge.* Banyan Botanicals. https://www.banyanbotanicals.com/info/blog-the-banyan-insight/details/rice-porridge/

Brown, P. (2017, September 5). *Handle the transition from Spring to Summer with Ayurveda*. Maharishi AyurVeda News & Knowledge. https://www.maharishi.co.uk/blog/handle-the-transition-from-spring-to-summer-with-ayurveda/

Carlson, L. H. (2018, April 4). *Yoga for Your Dosha: A Refreshing Pitta Yoga Sequence*. Yoga Journal. https://www.yogajournal.com/practice/yoga-for-dosha-refreshing-pitta-yoga-sequence#gid=ci02075695b00125bd&pid=larissa-hall-carlson-eye-of-the-needle-pose-variation-larissa-carlson

Caruthers, C. (2014, February 13). *10 Vata-Busting Ways to Own A Brutal Winter*. DOYOU.COM. https://www.doyou.com/10-vata-busting-ways-to-own-a-brutal-winter/

Carver, L. (2020, August 11). *Healthy Habits for Kapha Season*. Chopra. https://chopra.com/articles/healthy-habits-for-kapha-season

Collings, T. (2018, March 17). *AYURVEDA & THE SEASONS: SPRING*. Paavani Ayurveda. https://paavaniayurveda.com/blogs/the-ayurvedic-lifestyle/ayurveda-the-seasons-spring

CorePower Yoga. (n.d.). *CorePower Yoga*. Retrieved September 8, 2020, from https://www.corepoweryoga.com/blog/vata-balancing-poses-winter

Delight Yoga. (n.d.). *Kapha Season: How to stay warm and vibrant this winter | Delight Yoga*. Retrieved September 8,

2020, from https://delightyoga.com/blog/ayurveda/kapha-season-how-to-stay-warm-and-vibrant

Eckhart Yoga. (n.d.-a). *How to do Warrior 2 Pose-Virabhadrasana II-Ekhart Yoga | Ekhart Yoga.* Retrieved September 8, 2020, from https://www.ekhartyoga.com/resources/yoga-poses/warrior-ii-pose

Eckhart Yoga. (n.d.-b). *Warrior 1 Pose |Virabhadrasana 1 | Ekhart Yoga | Ekhart Yoga.* Retrieved September 8, 2020, from https://www.ekhartyoga.com/resources/yoga-poses/warrior-i-pose

Edwards, M. (2017, August 17). *How to Balance Pitta Dosha.* Living Ayurveda. https://qatoqi.com/ayurveda/blog/balancing-pitta-dosha/

Edwards, M. (2019, May 29). *How to Balance Vata Dosha.* Living Ayurveda. https://qatoqi.com/ayurveda/blog/balancing-vata-dosha/

Everyday Ayurveda. (2016a, September 1). *Kapha Diet and Recipes.* Ayurveda | Everyday Ayurveda. https://everydayayurveda.org/kapha-diet/

Everyday Ayurveda. (2016b, September 1). *Vata Diet and Recipes.* Ayurveda | Everyday Ayurveda. https://everydayayurveda.org/vata-diet-recipes/

Halpern, M. (2017, April 12). *Ayurveda and Asana: Yoga Poses for Your Health.* Yoga Journal. https://www.yogajournal.com/lifestyle/ayurveda-and-asana

Health and Hygiene. (n.d.). *Health + Hygiene.* Paavani Ayurveda. Retrieved September 8, 2020, from https://paavaniayurveda.com/collections/health-hygiene

Hip and Healthy. (2019a, June 19). *Summer Veggie Spring Rolls | Recipes | Hip And Healthy.* Hip & Healthy. https://hipandhealthy.com/summer-veggie-spring-rolls/

Hip and Healthy. (2019b, August 12). *6 Recipes For Your Kapha Dosha | Ayurvedic Recipes | Hip And Healthy.* Hip & Healthy. https://hipandhealthy.com/recipes-for-your-kapha-dosha/

Lad, U. L. V. (2018, December 20). *Hot Spiced Chai.* Banyan Botanicals. https://www.banyanbotanicals.com/info/blog-the-banyan-insight/details/hot-spiced-chai/

Lutzker, T. (2017a, April 5). *Stay Warm and Nourished.* Yoga Journal. https://www.yogajournal.com/uncategorized/stay-warm-and-nourished

Lutzker, T. (2017b, April 12). *Ayurvedic Spring Clean Eating Plan.* Yoga Journal. https://www.yogajournal.com/blog/spring-clean

Maharishi Ayurveda. (n.d.). *Kapha Balancing Water : Recipes | Maharishi Ayurveda.* Retrieved September 8, 2020, from

https://www.mapi.com/ayurvedic-recipes/spice-mixtures/
kapha-balancing-water.html

Maharishi Ayurveds. (n.d.). *Winter Pasta for Vata : Recipes | Maharishi Ayurveds*. Retrieved September 8, 2020, from https://www.mapi.com/ayurvedic-recipes/pasta/winter-pasta-for-vata.html

McCall, T. (2017, April 5). *Slow Down With Yoga for Vata Balance*. Yoga Journal. https://www.yogajournal.com/lifestyle/back-in-balance-2

mindbodygreen. (2020, May 14). *3 Ayurvedic Recipes For Early Summer (Cucumber Coconut Curry, Anyone?)*. https://www.mindbodygreen.com/articles/3-ayurvedic-lunch-and-dinner-recipes-for-early-summer

Mischke, M. (2020a, January 30). *Winter for Pitta*. Banyan Botanicals. https://www.banyanbotanicals.com/info/ayurvedic-living/living-ayurveda/seasonal-guides/winter-guide/winter-guide-pitta/

Mischke, M. (2020b, January 30). *Winter for Vata*. Banyan Botanicals. https://www.banyanbotanicals.com/info/ayurvedic-living/living-ayurveda/seasonal-guides/winter-guide/winter-guide-vata/

Morningstar, A. (2018a, October 2). *Baked Apples*. Banyan Botanicals. https://www.banyanbotanicals.com/info/blog-the-banyan-insight/details/baked-apples/

Morningstar, A. (2018b, December 20). *Maple Tapioca*. Banyan Botanicals. https://www.banyanbotanicals.com/info/blog-the-banyan-insight/details/maple-tapioca/

Morningstar, A. (2038, January 19). *Kapha-Pacifying Recipe: Fruit Crumble*. Banyan Botanicals. https://www.banyanbotanicals.com/info/blog-the-banyan-insight/details/kapha-fruit-crumble/

Nagabandhu. (2018, February 27). *Find here 6 Winter Yoga Poses including Lifestyle Tips for Activation*. https://www.livingpractice.life/nagabandhuyoga/?p=819

Pande, K. (n.d.). *Pitta spring wellbeing*. Pukka Herbs. Retrieved September 8, 2020, from https://pukkaherbsuswebsite.azurewebsites.net/your-wellbeing/stories/wellbeing/pitta-spring-wellbeing/

Pukka. (n.d.-a). *Pitta autumn wellbeing guide*. Retrieved September 8, 2020, from https://www.pukkaherbs.com/uk/en/wellbeing-articles/pitta-autumn-wellbeing-guide.html

Pukka. (n.d.-b). *Vata winter wellbeing guide*. Retrieved September 8, 2020, from https://www.pukkaherbs.com/uk/en/wellbeing-articles/vata-winter-wellbeing-guide.html

Pukka. (n.d.-c). *Winter wellbeing guide*. Retrieved September 8, 2020, from https://www.pukkaherbs.com/us/en/wellbeing-articles/winter-wellbeing-guide.html#:%7E:text=The%20dominant%20qualities%20present%20during,digestion%2C%20chills%20and%20swollen%20joints.

Quistgard, N. (2017, April 12). *Balancing Excess Pitta.* Yoga Journal. https://www.yogajournal.com/lifestyle/fired

Shah, N. (2038, January 19). *Kapha-Pacifying Recipe: Winter Elixir.* Banyan Botanicals. https://www.banyanbotanicals.com/ info/blog-the-banyan-insight/details/winter-elixir/

Sinclair, B. (2018, April 13). *Balancing Pitta for a More Peaceful Autumn.* Banyan Botanicals. https://www. banyanbotanicals.com/info/blog-the-banyan-insight/details/ balancing-pitta-for-a-more-peaceful-autumn/

Snyder, C. K. N. (2017, June 6). *Elemental Yoga: An Airy Asana Sequence to Balance Kapha.* Yoga Journal. https:// www.yogajournal.com/practice/elemental-yoga-airy-asana-sequence-balance-kapha-dosha#gid= ci02075695a01225bd&pid=plank-pose

The Art of Living. (n.d.). *3 Ways to Balance Your Kapha Dosha in Late Winter-Early Springs.* Art of Living (United States). Retrieved September 8, 2020, from https://www. artofliving.org/us-en/3-ways-to-balance-your-kapha-dosha-in-late-winter-early-springs

The Holistic Highway. (2020, January 14). *Springing into Spring Foods For Your Dosha.* https://theholistichighway. com/springing-into-spring-foods-for-your-dosha/

Tran, P. (2015, April 12). *How to Practice Kapalabhati Pranayama in Yoga.* YogaOutlet.Com. https://www.yogaoutlet.com/blogs/guides/how-to-practice-kapalabhati-pranayama-in-yoga

Very Well Fit. (n.d.). *How to Do Bow Pose (Dhanurasana) in Yoga.* Retrieved September 8, 2020, from https://www.verywellfit.com/how-to-do-bow-pose-techniques-benefits-variations-4690032

YJ Editors. (2017a, April 12). *Beginner's Guide to Pranayama.* Yoga Journal. https://www.yogajournal.com/practice/pranayama

YJ Editors. (2017b, April 12). *Standing Forward Bend.* Yoga Journal. https://www.yogajournal.com/poses/standing-forward-bend

YJ Editors. (2019a, January 7). *Bow Pose.* Yoga Journal. https://www.yogajournal.com/poses/bow-pose

YJ Editors. (2019b, January 7). *Garland Pose.* Yoga Journal. https://www.yogajournal.com/poses/garland-pose

Made in the USA
Coppell, TX
30 December 2020